A Sinner Saved by Grace in God's Hand

RON KINGSBURY

ISBN 978-1-0980-6145-6 (paperback)
ISBN 978-1-0980-6944-5 (hardcover)
ISBN 978-1-0980-6146-3 (digital)

Copyright © 2020 by Ron Kingsbury

All rights reserved. No part of this publication may be reproduced, distributed, or transmitted in any form or by any means, including photocopying, recording, or other electronic or mechanical methods without the prior written permission of the publisher. For permission requests, solicit the publisher via the address below.

Christian Faith Publishing, Inc.
832 Park Avenue
Meadville, PA 16335
www.christianfaithpublishing.com

Printed in the United States of America

To my wife, Joyce and our five children,
Debora Mark, John Sara, and Barbara

CHAPTER 1

I was born March 26, 1937, in Pontiac, Michigan, to Herbert Frederick Teak and Myrtle Ruth Ashley Teak. When I was three years old, living in a hotel in Port Huron, Michigan, my parents were separated and the court directed, after a divorce battle, my brother (David, age two) and I would live four months with each parent and with Grandma and Grandpa Teak in Oxford, Michigan.

I remember Grandpa Teak would drive to father's home and pick up David and I. Grandpa would sit on the back porch and Grandma would sit in her home in a rocking chair, watching people passing by or watch the traffic. They both had separate bedrooms. Grandma was always reading her Bible in her room. On Sunday we would walk to the Methodist Church for Sunday school and church.

When I was seven years old, I lived with my mother, and we lived in a small home in the north part of Port Huron. The house was one block from the cemetery where David and I played at night. Mother had a very short lady named Mrs. Horn who took care of us while mother worked. I would take the city bus to school. One day, on my way home from school, I had to cross the street which I did in front of the bus. I stepped in front of a car and was hit and I went right into a snowbank. I was okay but upset with the person driving the car.

When I was with father, he lived in a new town each time I was with him. He worked, building homes as a mason. After being divorced, he married my stepmother, Faye, and they had two children by the time I was twelve years old. That time we lived in Vassar, Michigan. I sold newspapers and delivered them on my bike. When I was thirteen, I called my mother to pick me up as I wanted to live with her. She and her boyfriend Joe Kingsbury picked me up, and we went home in Sparlingville, a suburb of Port Huron.

Joe took me to his church, The Salvation Army. I started to play the baritone horn, sang in the youth choir, attended Bible classes, and became a soldier of The Salvation Army. Phil played his baritone next to me. He worked for London Dairy delivering milk to homes in Port Huron. On Sunday, he picked me up at six thirty, and I helped him in delivering milk so that he could get to church on time. My pay was drinking cholate milk. Mother and Joe married and we became a great family.

When I started junior high school in Marysville, I took the last name as Kingsbury. I carried the name into high school in Port Huron. In both schools I played in their marching band with the baritone horn and held the first chair.

When I was sixteen, I set pins in a bowling alley. I had two lanes to place bowling pins in a rack after each bowling ball knocked the pins down. At the end of the frame I would push the rack to the floor and release the pins. Mother bowled on a league in this bowling alley. She had a problem with the gutter. To help her, I would set the bowling pens in the gutter. When I was seventeen, I worked for the Western Union. I would ride my bike all around Port Huron, delivering telegrams.

When I was sixteen, I joined the Michigan National Guard and started as a cook. This was a week before I turned seventeen. When I went to camp for training with our unit, I had my first day of being a cook. Our mess sergeant had me make a large pot of lemonade and I grabbed a brown bag of salt instead of a brown bag of sugar. That was the end of my cooking career. Upon the return from camp, I became a clerk typist for the Battalion S-1 (administration). I was promoted to corporal and served until I joined the US Army.

When I was eighteen, a senior in high school, I was walking down the hall and I saw a great-looking girl coming down the stairs. I stopped her and realized that we had met before. That is how I met

Joyce Hudson. She was the tomboy in our block back home where we lived before this day. She was a junior. She was walking home after school, which was three miles from the school. I said that I would walk with her as my home was over a mile from the school.

As we started walking home, I stopped in the middle of an alley and said, "Joyce, I will not take another step until you kiss me."

She did and started carrying my books. Joyce took the city bus to school and walked by the armory. She would watch me put up the United Sates flag at the National Guard Amory, which was a city block from the high school. Then we would walk to school.

For my senior prom, she was my date. Dad said I could use the car, but I found out he would be late. I called Joyce and explained what happened. Her father told me I could use his car. He picked me up so I could use the car. I had a flower for her dress and we left for this first date. At my prom, which was in Canada, I spent most of it sick (nerves). My best friend, *Don,* danced with Joyce and drove her home after they dropped me off at my home.

CHAPTER 2

A month before graduation, I visited the Army recruiter, and he developed a program for me and Wayne Lange under the buddy concept. I signed up for a four-year enlistment. We had basic training at Fort Leonard Wood, Missouri, together, and I was scheduled to go to the Adjutant General School at Fort Ben Harrison, Indianapolis, Indiana. Three days after graduation from high school, I said goodbye to Joyce and my parents and took a Greyhound bus with Wayne to Fort Leonard Wood.

After basic training, I was informed that I would attend eight weeks typing school at Ford Leonard Wood (not Fort Ben Harrison), and I had two weeks at home before going to typing school. Wayne went to airborne training. I went home for a two-week vacation before second training as a clerk. I went to see Joyce. Her mother told me that she was out with Don. Don told her that being a soldier, I would start drinking and using curse words. I waited until Joyce came home. When she walked in, she ran to me, jumped into my arms (the uniform did it), and Don left and never returned. After the vacation was over, Joyce went with me on the bus to Detroit. I had a layover for two hours, so we visited in a coffee shop and in the bus station until I got on the bus to Atlanta, Georgia, and then to Fort Leonard Wood.

When I completed the typing course my orders reflected, I would report to Fort Lewis, Washington, for taking a ship transport to the Far East Command. I asked about the Adjutant General

School at Fort Ben Harrison, AG, school. I was told that I just completed it at the clerk typing school.

Wayne Lange and I joined the Army together, under the buddy plan, so we could be together. We went to high school together and also members of the Michigan National Guard. Upon completion of our training, he went to Germany while I went to the Far East.

Mother and Joyce visited me at Fort Leonard Wood before I departed. Joyce and I talked about getting married, but I said that Korea is a *one-year* tour, and she would be able to complete high school. When Joyce returned home, her mother expected her to be married. They left the next day and I left for Fort Lewis, Washington.

Since I had a four-year enlistment, I had separate orders from the other class members going to Fort Lewis. When I went through orientation, I was given boarding number 11 for the ship roster. I worked as a clerk typist on the ship in the admin section for the troops. When the ship arrived in Yokohama, Japan, the command directed the boarding numbers from 1 to 12 to take their duffle bag and depart the ship.

A vehicle picked me up when I got off the ship and took me to Tokyo, assigned to the United Nations and Far East Command, enlisted detachment at Hardy Barracks. I reported to the 1SG and he showed me my desk as the detachment clerk. In my first letter to Joyce, I told her that I arrived in Japan and will be here for *three years*.

My first Sunday, I attended the chapel service at Hardy Barracks. Chaplain Hicks conducted a great service and I found my home. I became very active in the service as singing in the choir, ushering, and serving the communion. We would have Bible service and had a group called Protestant men of the chapel where I had visited with other groups. Once a month we would meet at the main chapel of Tokyo.

One Sunday, I took Gene Stahl with me to the chapel, and he noticed a young girl at the service. He asked me who she was, and I said her name was Fran and she was the chaplain's daughter. After I brought them together, they dated, and a year later, they got married. Gene was our personnel clerk.

I received a phone call from the command legal department, and they directed me to come to their office. The 1SG told me to report right away. Upon my arrival, I was informed the *Teak* family notified the Army that I entered the Army under a fraud name *Kingsbury*. The Legal Officer researched the law of Michigan pertaining to my name change. I informed him how I used the name through six years of schooling, The Salvation Army, and the National Guards for two years. The officer said the State of Michigan recognizes the individual as the name that he is known by.

Joyce and I sent letters every day. I would tell her about my job as detachment clerk and about friends of mine, which I got to know as I was also the mail clerk. In my second year in Japan, I met Michiko who sang in the chapel choir. We became friends during chapel functions. One day, she took me to her home, and I met her parents and two sisters. Her older sister was a medical doctor and both of her parents were dentist. Michiko was attending a medical college. My letter writing to Joyce started to slow down, and then they stopped, but Joyce did not give up hope, and I still received a letter a day.

Michiko and my relationship continued for a year and a half. I asked her if she would marry me. She said yes. She completed the application for marriage, which was approved by the Army. It was going well between us until her father said that we could not see each other, as he felt she would leave with me when I left Japan. I never saw her after that.

With six months to go before I returned to the States, Joyce still sent me a letter a day. I called Joyce from Japan, and then I started to send letters. Her mother sent me a letter after the phone call and told me how Joyce ran to her bed and jumped all around and reflected she never gave up on me. In a couple of months, I sent Joyce her engagement ring and I called her and asked her to marry me. She said yes, and we set the date for December 6, 1958.

CHAPTER 3

Upon completion of my tour in Japan, I received orders for my assignment to Walter Reed Army Hospital, Washington DC. I traveled on the same ship that I took to Japan and was assigned as a typist again. We stopped in Hawaii for one day and then to Los Angeles, going under the Golden Gate Bridge.

On November 11, 1958, I flew to Detroit Airport. When I went to the luggage area, I saw mother and Joyce carrying baby Ardelle (my brother's daughter). What a great sight.

Joyce and I got married on December 6 at Faith Lutheran Church in Port Huron and on to the honeymoon. We drove to Indiana and spent a couple of days with Uncle Don (a Methodist pastor) and Aunt Fran. After visiting for a couple of days, we traveled to Santa Claus, Indiana, and visited Santa's workshop and then on to Niagara Falls, drove across Canada and back to Port Huron.

After we returned home, Joyce, Mother, Stepfather, and I went to court to change my last name to Kingsbury by a judge. The judge asked Joe if I could use his name. When he said yes, he became *Dad*. Need to note that Dad was thirteen years older than I and he became a big brother and a great dad.

Joyce and I loaded up our 1957 Dodge and traveled to Washington DC.

I reported in at the hospital, and then Joyce and I searched for an apartment. We found a one-bedroom apartment, which was furnished. Rent was $97 a month. I was assigned as a personnel specialist. Our personnel sergeant had a PFC to give me a tour of the hospital. The PFC told me that I must do what he says. He told me to get my jacket and follow him. He was not a happy PFC when he saw I was two grades above him. One day, I was walking down a hallway in the hospital and met *Winston Churchill* from England and *President Eisenhower* as they were visiting someone in the hospital.

While I was assigned to Japan, I was promoted to specialist E-5 and had full benefits for Joyce. It was a good thing for her, as in a month, she went to the hospital and found out that Debora was on her way as the Army's first dependent for the Kingsbury family. She was born on August 20, 1959. Joyce and I joined a bowling league at the hospital bowling center. We moved into government quarters and lived there for a year and a half.

CHAPTER 4

After I served two years at Walter Reed Army Hospital, I received orders assigning me to 10th Field Hospital. Wurzburg, Germany. Joyce took Debbie to live with her parents until she received movement orders. I went to New York and departed on the same ship that I had traveled to Japan and back to the states. The ship arrived in Bremerhaven, Germany, and then I traveled by train to Wurzburg. I reported to the 1SG, where I was promoted to SGT E-5 and was assigned as personnel sergeant with a staff of seven enlisted personnel. Chief Warrant Officer Veder was my supervisor.

Three months later, Joyce got her passport and movement orders. She and Debora flew to Germany, and I met them at a military airport in Frankfort. Government quarters were not available yet, so we lived in a German home for four months. One morning, Joyce put Debora in a stroller and decided to meet me at the hospital. After walking an hour, she decided she was lost, so she followed her route back to the house. When I got home, we got in the car, and she showed me where she turned around to go home. I showed her if she continued about fifty yards, she was home again. She went in a circle to visit me.

We were assigned quarters on the third floor, across from the post elementary school. We attended the post Chapple. Debora was three years old and enjoyed Sunday school, which was in the elementary school. Joyce became a Sunday school teacher, and I became the Sunday school superintendent. Joyce also served as a Cub Scout den mother, and I became a Cub Scout master for two years. Joyce and I were very active in the NCO club (for grades E4–E9). Our tour was for three years and then extended for one more year.

Our neighbor across the hall was Sergeant Reggie Bayonne Sanderson and his wife, Lettie. He was a medical sergeant at the hospital. He would babysit with Deb. Joyce would receive a full medical report on our daughter each time he would take care of her.

Joyce and I learned that Wayne Lang and his family were stationed in Manheim, Germany. We visited him and met Jan and their children. We found they had the only A&W Root Beer stand in Germany where we obtained a gallon of root beer and took it home with us.

One Sunday, I was very ill and asked Debora to take my Sunday school records to the office, which was in the elementary school across the street from our quarters. She said "okay" and took the material. I received a call from the hospital duty NCO, who informed me that Debora wanted to get into my office. The hospital was a mile from our quarters. Debora was seven years old, and her only complaint was that it was a long walk and no one gave her a ride.

I was nominated for promotion to SSG E-6 and appeared before the promotion board. Mike, our company 1SG, recommended against my promotion, as he felt I was not qualified as I was too young. The hospital SGM recommended that I attend the 7th Army NCO Academy course for four weeks. The 1SG. agreed for me to go. *If I complete the course*, he said that he would pin on my stripes. He received a call from the academy asking him if he would attend the graduation as I was number 3 in the class. I received my promotion.

The NCO Club on the base decided to put on a fashion show. We announced the club would have topless waiters. When the night of the show arrived, the club was packed. Out came the topless waiters, all men. The fashion show was all men. I was dressed as a pregnant model. When my dance came up, I danced and sat on the lap of the hospital sergeant major.

Joyce and I provided another Army dependent with the birth of Mark Frederick on October 21, 1961.

We took a group trip to Paris, France, for four days at the cost of $25 per person. We took many tours around Paris, and it was great. Joyce soon found out that trip provided the Army another dependent.

CHAPTER 5

About ten months before we were to return to the states, I decided to try to become an officer. I took the tests and found that I was qualified and accepted for training at Fort Benning, Georgia. I received my assignment orders, and Joyce was in her eighth month. We cleared quarters, took our car to the port for shipment, lived in a German hotel, and still waited for shipment orders. The last day that Joyce could fly, we received our orders. We flew to McGuire Air Force Base, New Jersey, and I went to Newark to pick up our car and then back to the base to pick up Joyce, Debora, and Mark and headed to Michigan.

Once the family was settled in with Joyce's parents, I left for Fort Benning and was assigned to the Officers Candidate School on March 15, 1964. The first week was bad for new cadets. John Kingsbury became a dependent to the Army on March 19, 1964. After our last class for the day, my TAC Officer had us do two laps around the airborne track. When we were back to our barracks, while in formation, the TAC Officer informed the class that John was born and he and Joyce were doing great. In honor of John, we had to do two more laps.

At the end of eleven weeks, we had a class party, and Joyce came to Fort Benning to join me by bus. We had two days together and then back to training. On our eighteenth week, we became senior cadets and wore blue scarves and blue helmets. We could walk around the area and receive all authority over lower cadets, same as the officers.

At the end of twenty-three weeks of training, I received my commission as second lieutenant, as an Infantry Officer. Joyce's parents drove Joyce and the kids to see me receive my commission. Joyce and her mother pinned my second lieutenant bars on my uniform. SGT. Reggie Bayonne Sanderson was at my graduation and received my first salute from an enlisted man. I presented him with a one-dollar bill for my first salute.

Upon graduation, I received orders assigning me to the 1st Battalion, 41st Infantry Regiment, First Brigade, 2nd Armored Division Fort Hood, Texas, with training in a motor officer's class at Fort Knox Kentucky before going to Fort Hood. The class was eight weeks long. When I drove through the front gate of Fort Knox, a medical battalion was there, and on the command staff sign was the commander and SGM. Mike (my first sergeant in Germany). I entered the battalion command building, and a young man called the soldiers to attention (my first as an officer). I told them in a command voice to carry on and asked for the SGM Mike came out of his office, and we were reunited, and I sure felt great for the moment being above his rank. Joyce and I, with the children, visited him and his family that evening. We rented a trailer near Fort Knox that was furnished. John slept in a dresser drawer. Ron Mach and his wife, Sharon, lived in the trailer park with us. Ron was a classmate with me, where we were trained to be motor officers.

CHAPTER 6

In December, we arrived at Fort Hood and bought a home in Copperas Cove, Texas, three bedrooms, for $11,000. Furnished the home, put Debora and Mark in school, and I reported in at Fort Hood. I reported to LTC. Mace, and he appointed me as adjutant (S-1) to the battalion (no motor pool).

After a year in this position, I requested for transfer from Infantry Branch to the Adjutant General Corps, which was approved.

The Battalion Sergeant MAJ was in the hospital when I arrived. He had some visitors that informed him how a new second lieutenant was looking at the files and duty rosters. He was upset until he returned and found I was not a new officer out of college and had prior service in personnel. We became great friends after that. I received a letter from our supply officer (S-4) for the colonel to sign. I found several mistakes in the format of a military letter. I marked many errors and returned for retype. The CPT. took the letter and went right to LTC. Mace and complained about me correcting his letter. He left the office and I never saw him again.

Later on, that year our battalion was asked to conduct basic training for new soldiers. When they arrived, I took them to the local barbershop to remove all of their hair.

I served in that position for eighteen months. I learned to take an active membership of the Officer's Club. Joyce and I had a to attend official affairs at the club. We would bring the children there for brunch and swimming in the club swimming pool. Joyce and I went to the club for a New Year's party.

On New Year's Day, we were required to visit at the home of Battalion commander and followed with a visit the home of the Brigade commander and then on to the home of the Division commander. We would visit each one for thirty minutes, dressed in my formal uniform (*dress blues*). This policy was followed even in the headquarters US Army Europe.

The III Corps Headquarters sent a request to the 2nd Armored Division for an officer to be assigned to LTG(3 stars) Haines as his protocol officer. I was promoted to first lieutenant and was asked by the division if I would accept the position. I went for an interview with COL. Howard and was assigned. The battalion had a farewell ceremony for me and presented me an Army Commendation award.

I was responsible for official functions and events at the Officer's Club for General Haines. I was informed that there would be a few events for Lt. General Haines, as there would be a few visitors. Within a few weeks, the guests started to come in. I had to set up a dinner for each one and coordinated with Officers' Club staff. I would make a seating chart according to protocol. I would start with the General, his wife, and the honored guest. From there, I would seat other attendees according to their rank. Within six weeks, we hosted the Commanding General, 5th Army Command, the office of the Army Secretary of Defense, the Secretary of the Army, and the Army Chief of Staff. Lieutenant General Haines was promoted to general.

Joyce and I added the Army's fourth dependent. Sara was born at Darnell Army Hospital on March 17, 1966. We attended Trinity Lutheran Church in Copperas Cove, Texas. We sang in the choir, served as ushers, and I was a member of the church board.

CHAPTER 7

I received orders for Vietnam with MACV, III Corps Advisory section, Bien Hoe. I left Fort Hood in November 1966. I was assigned as assistant admin officer in the III Corps Advisory Headquarters. I was promoted to captain with eight officers from my OCS class. I assisted our chaplain whenever I could. I was responsible for the admin office, sending mail to the personnel in the field by air, a translator pool, a typing pool and interpreters.

I visited a medical headquarters in Bien Hoe Air Force Base and saw CWO Veder in the personnel section. He was my supervisor in Wurzburg, Germany. His personnel sergeant was Gene Stahl (assigned with me in Japan). Also visiting was three of the sergeants that were on my promotion board in Germany. We had a great reunion.

I took a USO Show "The Ink Spots" to Bien Hoe Air Force Base for transport to a field unit. The helicopters arrived to pick them up. Their pilot was MAJ. Ron Mach. We had a short reunion.

My boss was CPT. Allan Heard. Al and I would visit around Army or Air Force bases with two wonderful ladies. Alice was Al's girlfriend and MAJ. Pat Foote was her roommate. Thy were assigned at Camp Long Binh, US Army Vietnam Headquarters. We went to dinner two or three times a week depending which officer's mess had steak. Al went to Texas for a short visit and saw Joyce and the children.

Our office was responsible to coordinate the visits of many stars that would visit our military units.

My first night in Vietnam, someone was playing the piano. I was told that Martha Ray was playing. She was with us for many months. She wanted to visit all of the soldiers. On Christmas Eve, she had all of the personnel go to the dining room and she performed for us. After two hours, she said drinks at the clubs were on her. When she passed away, the government authorized for her to be laid to rest with the soldiers in a national cemetery. I was with Al as we visited with Henry Fonda, Chuck Connors, Jane Mansfield, Johnathan Winters, and Robert Mitchem. Billy Graham and his team had service for us which I attended with many service personnel.

One of my civilian translators was having a wedding which Al and I attended. After the service, we sat down for dinner. First course was chicken soup. When I was served, I received the chicken head. It was a great honor to receive it according to their tradition.

I was assigned a bed in the officers' quarters above the club in train compound. I met our maid that cleaned the quarters, made the beds, and washed our uniforms every day. A net was over the bed to keep out bugs. In the dining hall, we were served our meals by Vietnamese ladies.

I was presented the Army Bronze Star medal when I left Vietnam. I returned from Vietnam in November 1967, just before Thanksgiving. Joyce and the children met me at Belton airport, about thirty miles from Fort Hood. What a great homecoming.

Joyce remained in Copperas Cove and took care of our family while I was gone. She remained active with the church. She helped the military wives in Copperas Cove whose husbands were in Vietnam.

CHAPTER 8

We rented out our house and moved to Indianapolis, Indiana. We moved into an apartment, and I reported to the Adjutant General School at Fort Ben Harrison to attend the advanced course for AG officers. That course lasted nine months. When I was taking a test on computers, Joyce was very sick and she went to the hospital. Just before I took the test, I called Joyce to see what the doctor said. Joyce told me that she had a nine-month flu (Barbara was on her way).

Uncle Don and Aunt Fran visited on a Sunday, and we asked them to stay for dinner. While they were visiting, Joyce prepared the dinner by going to COL. Sanders. While we were eating dinner, Uncle Don said, "Joyce, this chicken is great." Before she could respond, Debbie said, "Here is the box it came in," pointing to the wastebasket.

Maj. Alan Heard, Maj. Pat Foote, and Alice (from Vietnam Command) came to visit us. Al said that my assignment committee, the three of them, have decided I need to be assigned in Washington DC. Pat Foot retired from the Army as a Brigadier General.

Upon graduation, I received orders assigning me to the Pentagon with duty at Fort Holabird, in Baltimore, Maryland. I was assigned there as administrator for an intelligence unit. One of my responsibilities was the control of classified documents. The custodian for the documents departed a few months before I arrived. I took the document log of all classified documents and checked the accountability of them. Everything was accounted for but found the log was completed incorrectly. Over a long period of time, I typed a new log for all documents. When completed, I informed my supervisor, a LTC, that the log was completed and I hope we do not have an inspection from our headquarters for two years. I was informed that would not happen.

One afternoon I was informed by the LTC that he is going to retire from the Army. To ensure that everything is correct, he requested an inspection of the unit. A warrant officer (a grade between a noncommissioned officer and an officer) came to inspect our classified documents. When he finished, he said all okay and he wanted to see the old register. When he saw the old register, he called for an investigation of the control of documents.

A senior officer came to our unit to do an investigation. I was told to not come in the unit for a week.

Mom and Dad Hudson (Joyce's parents) took Joyce and I to New York for a couple of days while the investigation was being done. I was called in to report to the senior officer at the end of the week. I explained to him what action that I did and who assisted me. The question was about the use of pen entries on the documents. I said I had no idea who made the entries but I am responsible for them. My supervisor was told I said I was responsible. My supervisor said to the senior officer he knew Kingsbury was responsible for the errors. Then I was asked where I would like to be assigned to, I asked for Germany and was told okay. I received orders in September 1969 for assignment to Headquarters, US Army Europe Command, in Heidelberg, Germany.

On October 5, 1968, Barbara became the Army's fifth dependent to the Kingsbury family. She was born at Fort Meade, Maryland.

CHAPTER 9

I was further assigned as administrator for the intelligence staff of Headquarters US Army Europe. In a couple of months, Joyce arrived with the five children and we moved into government quarters in Patrick Henry Village. I was in Germany for five months when I received orders to report to Vietnam. Major General Foster sent a message to the Pentagon requesting that I remain in Germany which would be in the best interest for the Army. The orders to Vietnam were cancelled and Joyce and I stayed four years.

The Adjutant General of US Army Europe had a meeting with all of the admin officers. After the introductions of the staff, he asked for us to get to know each other and help when needed. One Sunday, after church service, Joyce and I, with five Army dependents, went to the Officer's Club brunch. While we were eating, Lt. Dotty (Admin Officer for engineer staff) came into the club and I introduced her to Joyce and the children. Debora asked her if she would like to go with us to the drive through zoo. She accepted and spent the day with us. She came to our quarters with us for dinner. After dinner, she played her guitar and sang to the children. She became Aunt Dotty. I would help her with her work at the Engineer Department. One of the projects was to write a directive pertaining classified documents. Our staff was able to assist her in the control of documents.

Her friendship did cause a concern for some of our neighbors. I received a call from Quarter Assignments Director saying that he received a phone call, informing him that Joyce and the children had

GOD'S PLAN

returned to the states. A red Volkswagen, belonging to Dotty, was parked at our quarters for a number of nights and I must move out of the quarters. I informed him that Joyce and the children were here and Dotty's parents are visiting and staying with us. Dotty's father is driving her car. They planned to visit and obtained their airplane tickets just before the dollar value dropped. They could not stay in a hotel and she lived in a two-room quarters.

Joyce and I, with Dotty, met Clement. He was a German soldier in World War II. He arranged the entertainment for the Officer's Club. We became close friends. He would join us at the club having brunch almost every Sunday after church services. Sometimes he came over to our quarters and had dinner. Clement loved corn on the cob, as in Germany, corn was cattle feed.

On many occasions, we went to his home to visit.

On Debora's twelfth birthday, Clement made a recording of her singing with a recording of a full band orchestra. She treasured that gift. Clement was able to do all recordings in his home. He recorded all the music for a TV series called *Lassie*. One Sunday, he called Joyce and told her that he was not able to come for dinner as Tom Jones was at his home.

During the war he was captured as a POW and brought to the states. When the war was over, he started arranging and recording Duke Ellington music as Clement was gifted with music. He also worked with Judy Garland and another artist. One year Clement was in an accident in Munich, Germany, and Judy got to the hospital before his wife arrived from Heidelberg.

Mother and Dad came to visit us in Germany. We took them to the Officer's Club for Sunday brunch. Clement came to the club and joined us. He was very quiet when he met Dad. He asked Dad if he was in Germany, was he with an engineer unit, and had a Mexican soldier with him. When Dad said yes to all the questions, Clement said, 'Sir, you were the American soldier that I surrendered to."

We took Mom and Dad to Luxemburg to visit the national cemetery where Gen. George Paton is at rest. I found that I locked the keys inside of the car, which got me a laugh from Dad. He got the car open. We also went to Munich and to the Bavarian Alps. After we got back to Heidelberg, Dad had a mild heart attack. He was admitted into the Army hospital. Ardle, my brother's daughter, had come with Mom and Dad and had a great visit with Debora being her guide.

CPT. Skip Baily was the aide to my general and lived in a building next to our building. December 6, 1972, I took Joyce to the Officer's Club to celebrate our wedding anniversary. While we were eating, Skip called me and asked if we could come to his quarters as his son was very sick and need to take him to the hospital. Before we left the club, he said that he and his wife were at our quarters to see if we had any ice to lower his temperature. Since we did not have enough ice, he needed to have me bring ice from the club. Joyce and I took a bag of ice and rushed home. When we arrived, we found a bunch of our friends as our daughter Deb and Skip had an anniversary party for us. His only problem was no ice. His son was not sick.

Joyce and I were very active in the housing area called Patrick Henry Village. We assisted at school functions for the five children. We were active in the chapel, singing in the choir. Joyce was Sunday school teacher, and I served as Sunday school superintendent. Joyce served as den mother and I served as Scout Master for the Cub Scouts pack in our housing area.

Once a year, a big carnival was set up for the youth of the village. It would start the last week of June and close on the Fourth of July with the fireworks. The staff of our headquarters would sponsor different events. The intelligence staff operated a large German beer tent.

The high school students would hang around the bowling alley. I drove to the grocery store, picked up few items. When I started for our quarters, I drove past the bowling alley and saw Debora with a cigarette in her hand. When she saw me, she panicked.

Our quarters had a room on the top floor (fourth floor) of our building for maid quarters. Debora asked if she could have some friends over for a slumber party. They would use the lounge upstairs. We said yes and Joyce had snacks for them. They would use our bathroom if needed. That Friday night fifteen girls came for the event. Joyce would check on them when needed. At the time Joyce and I would go to bed, our lights turned off, and we could see the reflection on the windows of the stairwell, across the parking area for the quarters next to us. The stairwell was showing the girls looking out at each floor. We then noticed a bunch of boys across the parking area. The girls took turns coming to the bathroom and asked when we were going to bed. We stayed up very late and watched the boys leaving one by one.

Debora attended confirmation classes for the Lutheran Church at our chapel. These classes last for one year, meeting once a week. Upon completion of confirmation classes, all Lutheran children in Germany met at Worms, Germany. Worms, Germany, is where Martin Luther debated to the Holy Roman Emperor and prince-bishops from districts around Germany in the year 1521. This meeting was in reference to the Reformation movement from the Catholic Church. The children attended their confirmation in the Romanesque Cathedral. Joyce's parents attended with us. It was a wonderful day.

CHAPTER 10

In July 1974, Joyce and I returned to the States with assignment to Fort Hood, Texas. We left from the Officers' Club with a sedan to the Air Force base. Clement and Dotty were there to see us off. When we arrived in good old USA, we stopped at Martinsburg, West Virginia, to visit Dottie's parents for a couple of days. Then we drove to Michigan to visit our families.

When I arrived at Fort Hood III Corps command assignment center, I was told Lt. Colonel White, Adjutant General, Second Armored Division requested that I be assigned to his office as Adjutant General Executive Officer. I had no idea who Colonel White was, but I reported as directed. When I saw the Colonel, in came Warrant Officer Gene Stahl (the same person with me in Japan and Vietnam). He was our chief of officer records.

On my first day in the office, I received a phone call from Colonel Marrow from the Army command (he was one of my supervisors in Germany). He said that he wanted me to work for him in Atlanta, Georgia, and not to unpack our things and orders will be on the way. When I informed him that I am required to retire from the Army on June 30, 1975, he said he could not justify the change to Atlanta for just eleven months.

Colonel White told me that he needs me to develop a field exercise of the Division Rear Command. When a division is at war, it has two brigades on the front line and one brigade in the Division Rear. The Division Adjutant General is the Commander of the Division Rear. The Brigades rotate during the campaign. As the executive

Officer, I had the responsibility to develop the Division rear exercise for the Second Armored Division.

Masters Command at Fort Hood is responsible for testing of all elements of III Corps. A MAJ was assigned to work with me. The first thing we did was to fly by helicopter to the State National Guard at Camp Mabry in Austin. We met with their operations department and flew by for helicopter to Camp Swift at Bastrop, Texas. They provided us with an area of warehouse buildings that would support this exercise. These buildings provided the following:

- The largest building provided a dining area and kitchen for feeding 550 personnel (Bergstrom AFB Commissary agreed to provide all rations); a medical clinic; a post exchange (which I was able to obtain services from Bergstrom Air Force Base in Austin); and an area for movies and recreational services.
- Enlisted and officers' personnel records. These records are for all the personnel assigned to the Second Armor Division.
- Military police company for security of the area
- Division postal services. Mail processed and delivered to units in the division
- Division replacement service for all personnel being assigned to the division
- Division finance department for payroll to all personnel of the division
- Sleeping quarters for all male personnel
- Sleeping quarters for all female personnel
- Parking of all vehicles inside when not being used

The following units were provided for support from the division:

- Medical unit to operate a medical clinic during exercise
- A shower unit with shower tent and equipment
- Computer support with punch cards

- Aviation unit to establish a control center for helicopters transporting from and to Fort Hood and Camp Swift
- Transportation unit to move all personnel, files, and equipment. This section obtained clearance from the state of Texas to move from Fort Hood to Camp Swift.

Two weeks before the exercise, COL. White and I took all of the officers involved in the exercise to Camp Swift. They toured the site and were assigned buildings for their sections. The representative from Bergstrom Air Force Base exchange was to show where the PX and laundry service would be located.

Brigadier General Goodwin, Deputy General, Second Armored Division, was with us during the exercise. COL. White and I lived in a house located on the site, which was our headquarters. A tent was set up in front of the house for briefings.

When the exercise starts under a simulated war event, Major General Fair, Commanding General of the Second Armored Division, flew in his helicopter and was met by two jeeps and military police for bodyguards. He was taken to the tent for briefing. I was introduced as the Mayor of Bastrop area. I briefed the General and his staff. He then took a tour of the buildings and saw their operations followed by dinner in the kitchen area.

The exercise was the last week of May 1975 and the first week of June 1975. This time was established to provide the finance department to pay all of the troops in the Second Armored Division at Fort Hood, on May 31.

Masters collected all of the data and reported that we had a great exercise. When we returned to Fort Hood, Colonel White told me that my replacement was assigned and for me to take off for two weeks and get ready for retirement.

On June 30, 1975, I retired from the US Army after twenty-two years of service. I reported to the division for my retirement in a large theater in the Second Armored Division as it was raining on the parade grounds. The division band was playing in the back of the building. The officers of the AG office were present as well as noncommissioned officers. My parents and Joyce's parents, Lt.

Dotty Stevens and her parents, and our friends were present to see my retirement service. General Goodwin conducted my retirement service and presented me the Army Distinguished Service Medal. I was informed that this award is presented to Generals and Field Grade Officers. Very few captains have received this award. After the service, we went to the Officers' Club for dinner.

CHAPTER 11

Start of our new life out of the service.

During my tour at Fort Hood, Joyce and I were very active with Faith Lutheran Church, being on the church board and helping with typing the church program every Saturday and helping the pastor. When I was moving to Austin, the pastor had a couple of church members place their hands on my head and prayed for me. What an emotional feeling that was.

In Killeen I went to Evins Personnel Employment Services and asked if I could work for the company. The manager sent me to Austin to visit Mrs. Evins. After the interview, she asked me to move to Austin and work at her office. I returned to Copperas Cove, and I informed Joyce about the offer. Within two weeks I became a personnel consultant for Evins. Every day I would drive back and forth. Mrs. Evins put me in touch with a real-estate lady and we bought a three-bedroom house. The Army had a moving company pack everything and moved everything to Austin. Joyce loaded the car with five children and met me at Holiday Inn for the night. The next day we moved into our new home.

We had life insurance policies with Lutheran Brotherhood, and Odis George became our insurance agent. We became good friends. After working with Evins for six months, I visited Walter Beglau who was the general manager for Lutheran Brotherhood. After visiting with him, I left Evins Personnel and became an insurance agent. I went through local training and training at their home office in Minneapolis, Minnesota. Odis and I worked together and I did very well. Walter was responsible for Texas, Oklahoma, Louisiana, and Mississippi. He had me become his insurance trainer for his agents, and I would travel to the areas.

One of my policy holders was Don Phillips. When I visited his home, he said he would obtain additional insurance if I would visit his Kiwanis club. I went with him to El Chico restaurant at Hancock Shopping Center and had lunch with the Austin North East Kiwanis Club. Within a couple of weeks, I joined the club. A year later, I got my first member to join, who was Odis George.

Walter had a training meeting with the agents and obtained an outstanding speaker about motivation. She called me to answer a few questions. First question was what have I wanted to be. I said a Lutheran pastor. Then she asked me what stopped me. I replied, money, family, education…etc. After some discussion, I was a student in Concordia Lutheran Junior College.

CHAPTER 12

When we moved to Austin, Joyce and I joined Redeemer Lutheran Church, Missouri Synod. The church had an elementary school for our children, which was great. I became Sunday School Director, and Joyce and I sang in the choir. The church gave me a scholarship toward Concordia education. I was in my final semester of the second year when I visited The Salvation Army with Major Hall. With my studies, I was offered a chance to council with the homeless clients which would be good training for me.

One day in 1979, I was called to the pastor's office of another Lutheran church. He informed me if I wanted to be a Lutheran pastor, I had to stop going to The Salvation Army. I quit the Church and Concordia. I visited the pastor of the St. Paul Lutheran Church at Concordia and I informed him what happened. He was also leaving the synod. He recommended that I visit Pastor Karl Grunberg at Gethsemane Lutheran Church. Joyce and I took the children to Gethsemane and visited Pastor Grunberg. The next week, our membership was transferred to Gethsemane, Evangelic Lutheran Church of America.

I informed Major Hall about my changes and asked if I could help with counseling. He said yes and I was given an office to work in. Mrs. Major Hall said that I should receive $100 a week. After two weeks, I became an employee, which lasted thirty-two years.

I started as a counselor and given an office above The Salvation Army store. I worked six days a week, visiting with the homeless and being present during the supper meal. Within a few weeks, I became the personnel director hiring and terminating the homeless that were working in the warehouse that received donations and operated a store where they sold the items at a very low price.

I met with Frank Deutsch, Austin Baptist Association, and Jerry Eichorn, Caritas Catholic Services. The three of us worked together serving the homeless. We started meeting once a week discussing the needs and what services were available for them. After working together around six months, we were joined by a representative of Travis County. After a couple of months later, a representative from the city of Austin joined us. We worked together for a number of years. Working together, the city opened an Austin Resource Center for the homeless. Caritas opened a soup kitchen serving meals to the homeless. Frank opened a Baptist kitchen serving noon meals as The Salvation Army served breakfast and supper. Frank also coordinated with grocery outlets receiving bulk food items and distributed them to the Austin Food Bank and other feeding agencies.

I received the responsibility of supporting disasters with a mobile canteen. Claud and his wife took care of the canteen and went to respond to fires, floods, and when requested by the fire chief, the city of Austin, and county judges of Travis County and Williamson County. He and his wife lived in low-cost housing and received a radio from the fire department so that they could respond when needed. He would call me and I would meet them at the disaster.

One day I was informed Claude had a heart attack and passed away to heaven. I was informed the fire department would take care of the funeral service. When I entered in the chapel, I saw two firemen next to the casket with a silver helmet on top. After the service, six firemen carried Claude to the back of number one firetruck. As we traveled the route to the cemetery, firetrucks lined the route with firemen standing next to their truck and saluted as we would go by them. When we started, two firetrucks extended their latter up and formed an arch as we passed under them.

Working with The Salvation Army Division Headquarters, we opened a halfway house for state and federal inmates. I hired a great person to manage the halfway house. He was responsible for insuring they would obtain employment and followed the rules established by state and federal paroles divisions.

One afternoon, I was at the reception area when this lady came in with a box of items she wanted to donate. I received the box and answered her questions about the facility and how we were doing. When she departed, I noticed a man waiting for her at the end of the sidewalk. I then realized she was Lady Bird Johnson. I gave the box to Major Hall.

CHAPTER 13

During my years with The Salvation Army, I met many homeless individuals. Many would visit me when they arrived in Austin for assistance. Every year I would manage the Red Kettle Campaign with homeless individuals with staff supervisor managing a team of fifteen bell ringers. I would have three teams every year; the current bell ringers would return. A great fellowship was developed with them.

I worked with many men and women and some with their families that were not homeless. Here is one case I will always remember. A lady was riding in a pickup truck and came for some help. Her story was she was concerned about her husband that was in an Army hospital in San Antonio and she was afraid of him. I had her visit with our social worker Ann. She left and thanked everyone; she came back with tubs and boxes of COL. Sanders' chicken dinner for the employees' supper. She said she was going back to her ranch and had a cook that has made her dinner and was not able to stay.

The next day, she came back and talked with Ann. She was more worried about her husband as someone put sugar in the gas tank of her truck. Ann and I talked with her, and she said she needed some place to stay, and it would be a few days. Bill, who operated our disaster canteen, and his wife were at the office and invited for her to stay with them. She left with them. A couple of days later, she came back to the office and said she could not stay with them and she had to sign her company paychecks which would be delivered at the airport in her private jet the next day.

I talked with my wife, Joyce, and then I invited her to stay with us for two days. She went with me to our home. Met Joyce and our kids and had a great visit. The next day, Joyce took me to work. When I came home, Joyce said she loaned her our car to go to the airport and would be back shortly.

When she returned, she had gifts for the children and sack lunches for them, made by her cook, for school the next day.

Again, Joyce took me to work, and when she needed to pick me up, she called and said the lady borrowed the car again and has not returned. I got a ride home and waited for her to bring the car home. She did not return. The next day I received a phone call from Taylor Police Department. They had our car, and the lady was arrested. She tried to cash a stolen check at one of their banks. After they arrested her, they found that she was wanted in five states for stolen credit cards, fraud, and for being a con artist. They found she had many stolen credit cards in her purse. In the trunk of the car, we found she made the lunches and left everything in the trunk.

The year 1980, we started to build a larger Salvation Army Social Service Center with the Area Command.

We moved out of a two-story house on Second Street with nine employees to a three-story center on Eighth Street with one hundred employees. I became the administrator for operations.

CHAPTER 14

Alan Ritson, the disaster director from The Salvation Army Division Headquarters in Dallas, Texas, came to Austin to attend a meeting with the state of Texas, Division of Emergency Management. He asked me to go with him to this meeting. The director of Texas Emergency Operation Center informed us that The American Red Cross asked not to be responsible for the mass care support for the state. After a good discussion, The Salvation Army took over the program of mass care.

I was designated the representative for The Salvation Army Division Headquarters. I was assigned a place in the operation center. When the center was open to support a state disaster, I would report to the office and open communication with The Salvation Army Division Headquarters. I would coordinate the needs of support from The Salvation Army.

I also represented The Salvation Army Austin Area Command at the Travis County/City of Austin Emergence Operation Center and Austin Alliance committee.

Different times, Captain Todd Smith from our division headquarters would join me in the center. One time that he was there, President Bush came in the operation center thanking the members supporting a disaster.

One of the disasters was the space vehicle that was destroyed on its entry to earth. I reported to the Emergency Operation Center to coordinate with Alan Ritson the needs from The Salvation Army. I informed him that the state has identified Lufkin, Texas, as the state operation center. Alan dispatched mobile canteens from Texas units, including our canteen from Austin, to go to Lufkin. The state was in the recovery of the crew members. Bill Duncan with his wife took our canteen to Lufkin. They provided drinks, meals, coffee, and doughnuts to the responders. After a couple of days, I needed to send replacements for Bill and his wife. I called our Kiwanis division Lt. Governor for Division 24 (Austin area) for volunteers. He said he and his wife would go and serve as long as they were needed. When I saw them when they returned, they said how well they did and felt honored that they could serve. His wife reflected that it touched her seeing an astronaut with tears when given a cup of coffee and doughnuts.

CHAPTER 15

I have found a great family of Kiwanis members in Texas and Oklahoma District on August 25, 1977.
Relationship that is second to none. We gather together at conventions, training for officers, council meetings, and club meetings.

I have served in many positions within our club and Kiwanis Texas/Oklahoma District:

- Club—vice president, president, secretary and treasurer (thirty-two years).
- Division 24—Lt. Governor
- Texas/Oklahoma District—secretary, chairman spiritual aims, chairman inter clubs, chairman club reports, and chairman for the (year 2000) district convention.

In 1998, our current Lt. Governor for Division 24 informed me that he went to the district convention and they approved a convention in Austin, year 2000. He had the event manager from the Double Tree Hotel. He was at the convention and has started to develop the hotel for the convention. I asked him if he could have the open session for over one thousand Kiwanis members and he said yes. I then asked him then the members could go directly in to their dinner meal in the hotel. He said they could not as they did not have the space. Our Lt. Governor called the district office and cancelled the convention for 2000.

I received a messaged from our governor elect of Tex/Okla District saying the convention must be held in Austin, and he wanted me to be the chairman of the convention. I visited all of the convention facilities in Austin and they were booked four years to seven years. A few weeks later the event manager of Double Tree Hotel informed me that the Red Lion Hotel was available for the same weekend. We will have a convention. Both hotels were in the same block.

I contacted all of the past Lt Governors as they had attended at least two conventions. All of the events were covered by them. Also, I appointed two co-chairmen to help me, one for finances and one for operations. We had one of the best conventions with over one thousand in attendance.

Our Kiwanis club work with The Salvation Army as:

- we assisted The Salvation Army ringing bells at their Christmas Kettles.
- we assisted The Salvation Army serving with their disaster program, serving on their disaster vehicle, serving meals and drinks to first responders and victims involved. Our club and Division 24 received training at The Salvation Army Area Command in food service. The area commander asked me to recruit volunteers to assist with disasters. I asked my Kiwanis club if they would help and they said yes. This project was started by our Kiwanis club and ended up at Texas/Oklahoma District of Kiwanis International. The District Past Lt. Governor's Association, President Barbara Johnson, took over the project for the district. The district, with The Salvation Army, provided training at their annual conventions and mid-winter conferences.

Our club projects include services for senior citizens, boy scouts, elementary schools reading to the children, and community services such as cleaning the highway.

CHAPTER 16

When I was working for The Salvation Army, I became closer to *my Lord,* and *God touched me and a new life began.* Through his love for me and the love of my wife and my family, I was able to give my life full time serving my Lord and my family with a new mind, new heart, a new body, and a new soul. I know that my past was forgiven as if it never happened. My hardest part was forgiving myself.

After I retired from The Salvation Army, I had three knee surgeries and a major infection in my body. I ended up with major medical problems which I lost control of my legs. I started to reflect on my life and realized how *GOD had the plans for my life.*

When I retired at Fort Hood, Texas, I was offered a great job. I was offered to be the director of retirement services at Fort Hood. God had other plans and I said no and moved to Austin based on faith.

With my time in the Army, I received great assignments as an enlisted man and an officer. I became a leader; I took responsibility for my actions, and my service to my God, country, and family.

When I retired, I received full benefits for Joyce and I plus a great retirement income for the rest of our life.

- I went to college to learn about my faith and service in the name of Christ.
- I went to college to learn social services procedures.

- I became an employee of The Salvation Army for thirty-eight years where we fed the homeless, provided them with shelter, and provided them with clothing. They received medical care, showers, laundry service, and counseling. I became the administrator for operations.
- We had a halfway house for federal and state prisoner, providing employment services and their basic services and counseling and transition into the community.

The greatest thing that was done by *our Lord* was bringing into my life Joyce Hudson. She became my partner, and we provided five wonderful children. Our family grew in the faith of Christ. Joyce took on a great love for me and our children. Her faith in our church was second to none. She had to move around the world, she had to manage the family for a year while I served in Vietnam, and she was at my side at all times. When she came down with cancer, she demonstrated her love for me and the family.

She colored pictures for all of the great grandchildren, she marked all of her possession for the children and great-grandchildren, and she had great concern on how I would continue my life without her. Joyce was promoted to glory on May 8, 2016.

One person that had a great impact on my faith was Pastor Karl Grunberg, Pastor, Gethsemane Lutheran Church, Austin Texas. Not only our pastor but a great counselor for our family, a brother in Christ, a personal friend, and a great Kiwanian. He renewed our marriage on our twenty-fifth wedding anniversary, married our five children, baptized our grandchildren and great-grandchildren, and conducted funeral services for five family members, including my partner that was promoted to glory. He attended family functions including Joyce's birthday party on October 19, 2015. When Karl would walk into our presence, you would feel the Lord being with us. One special event that took place in my life was when Karl called me up to the church altar and washed my feet in front of the congregation. I felt so humble.

On December 7, 1989, I had invited our Pastor Karl Grunberg to be our speaker with a Christmas message at our Kiwanis club.

Jack McGee, governor of Texas/Oklahoma District, Kiwanis International, visited our club that day. When Karl finished his message, he said, "Ron has been after me to become a member of this club. In honor of his wife, Joyce, I would like to join this club." I looked at our governor and asked him if he ever heard of a better application for membership and he said *no*. I called a quick board meeting and made the motion to accept his application and the club voted yes. I turned to Governor McGee and asked him if he would like to install a new member. He said yes and then he installed Karl, removed his Legion of Honor pin, and put it on Karl's lapel of his suit.

I know that our Lord speaks to us in many ways as we listen to his call through the Holy Spirit. One time he spoke to me in a dream in June 2017. In Acts 2:17, God said, "Young men will have visions and old men will have dreams."

One of my dreams was of me visiting The Salvation Army while Joyce sat in the car. When I returned to the car, Joyce wanted to go to the store. I took her to the store and returned to my office. I went back to pick Joyce up. When I called her, she was as young as she was when we got married, wearing her favorite blue coat. She said she wanted to go home. Driving down Sixth Street, we headed to Mopac. The next thing I knew, I was carrying Joyce in my arms. I told her that she was feeling cold to my touch. I laid her down and was told to go to a vacant lot downtown. I was taken to that place, and a few of our friends were there. Joyce stood among us when I saw a white cloud coming toward us with an opening in the middle. When I looked into the cloud as it was right above us, I saw wonderful colors of blue and gold. Then I saw *Joyce go up into the cloud,* and then a flash of a bright light appeared as we *watched her go into heaven*. What a true angel she is. I woke up and praised the Lord and cried with great joy.

> And when Jesus had spoken these things, while they beheld, *he was taken up; a cloud received him* out of their sight.

CPSIA information can be obtained
at www.ICGtesting.com
Printed in the USA
BVHW072249060121
597088BV00002B/166